48 HOCKEY
FUN FACTS, TRIVIA QUIZ & JOKES FOR
YOUNG CANADIANS

Dr. Fanatomy

© Copyright 2023-24 - All rights reserved.

The content contained within this book may not be reproduced, duplicated or transmitted without direct written permission from the author or the publisher.

Under no circumstances will any blame or legal responsibility be held against the publisher, or author, for any damages, reparation, or monetary loss due to the information contained within this book, either directly or indirectly.

Legal Notice:
This book is copyright protected. It is only for personal use. You cannot amend, distribute, sell, use, quote, or paraphrase any part, or the content within this book, without the author or publisher's consent.

Disclaimer Notice:
Please note the information contained within this document is for educational and entertainment purposes only. All effort has been executed to present accurate, up-to-date, reliable, complete information. No warranties of any kind are declared or implied. Readers acknowledge that the author is not engaged in the rendering of legal, financial, medical or professional advice. The content within this book has been derived from various sources. Please consult a licensed professional before attempting any techniques outlined in this book.

By reading this document, the reader agrees that under no circumstances is the author responsible for any losses, direct or indirect, that are incurred as a result of the use of the information contained within this document, including, but not limited to, errors, omissions, or inaccuracies.

Bonus Booklet For You!

With great pleasure, I warmly welcome you to purchase the book. Congratulations on stepping towards improving yourself and developing the skills necessary to thrive as a teenager and beyond.

Below is a surprise gift for you!

Download it from the link (or scan the QR code below) –
https://bit.ly/TeeNavigationBonus

Table of Contents

EACH CHAPTER CONTAINS:
part a: Fun Facts
part b: trivia quiz
part c: jokes

1. Introduction – History: Origin of the game (pg 1-10)

2. Legends of the Ice (pg 11-27)
- Wayne Gretzky: The Great One
- Bobby Orr: A Defenseman's Dream
- Maurice "Rocket" Richard: Scoring Sensation

3. Stanley Cup Glory (pg 28-40)
- The Quest for Lord Stanley's Cup
- Historic Stanley Cup Moments
- Canadian Dominance in the NHL

4. The Heroes' Journeys (pg 41-52)
- Kid Heroes of the NHL
- Rookie Sensations
- Young Players Who Captured Hearts

5. Puck Dreams on Canadian Soil (pg 53-64)
- Backyard Rinks and Frozen Ponds
- Learning to Skate and Shoot
- From Pick-Up Games to Organized Hockey

Table of Contents

6. The Spirit of Canadian Hockey (pg 65-75)
- Values and Traditions of the Game
- Sportsmanship and Teamwork
- The Role of Coaches and Mentors

7. Women in Canadian Hockey (pg 76-88)
- Hayley Wickenheiser: A Trailblazer
- Marie-Philip Poulin: Golden Moments
- Leading the Way for Female Players

8. Most exciting matches (pg 89-99)
- 1972 Summit Series: Canada vs. the Soviet Union
- Mario's Miracle: The 1987 Canada Cup Showdown
- The Golden Moment: 2010 Winter Olympics
- 2014 Sochi Olympics Men's Hockey Final
- 2016 World Cup of Hockey Final: Canada vs. Team Europe
- 2020 IIHF World Junior Championship Final: Canada vs. Russia

Trivia Quiz Solution (pg 100-108)

Conclusion (pg 109)

1. HISTORY: ORIGINS OF THE GAME

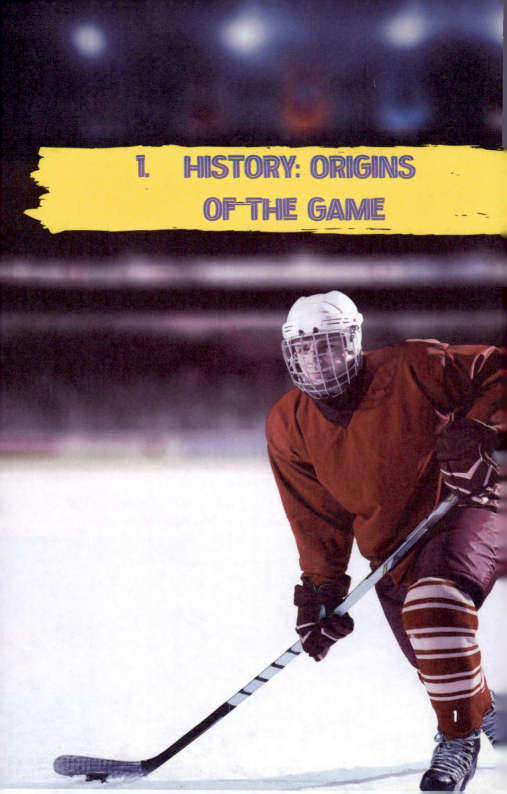

1. Frozen Roots:
The origins of hockey can be traced back to ancient times, with early forms of the game being played in civilizations like Egypt and Greece, where a ball was slapped with a stick.

2. Early Puck Provisions:
Before the rubber puck became standard, early hockey players used wooden balls, carved pieces of cork, or even frozen cow dung as makeshift pucks.

3. Nail-Biting Matches:
The first recorded organized indoor hockey game took place in Montreal, Canada, in 1875. The tournament was played at the Victoria Skating Rink, and the goals were two large 'nail' posts driven into the ice.

4. Hockey Stick Evolution:
Early hockey sticks were straight and made entirely of wood. The curved blade design that we see today became popular in the 1960s.

5. Origins of the Word 'Puck':
The term 'puck' is believed to have Scottish roots, derived from the Gaelic word "puc" or the Scottish Gaelic "poc," both meaning to poke or punch.

6. First Women's Hockey Game:

The first documented women's hockey game occurred in 1892 in Barrie, Ontario. The teams comprised members of the local Women's Christian Temperance Union.

7. The Birth of the Blue Line:

The blue lines on a hockey rink were introduced in 1918 by the NHL. Before this, players could stand anywhere on the ice, leading to frequent offside calls.

8. Hockey's Olympic Debut:

Ice hockey debuted at the 1920 Summer Olympics in Antwerp, Belgium. Canada dominated, winning gold and outscoring their opponents 29-1.

9. The First NHL Game:

The National Hockey League (NHL) played its first official game on December 19, 1917. The Montreal Canadiens faced off against the Ottawa Senators, with the Canadiens winning 7-4.

10. The Zamboni Invention:

The first ice resurfacing machine, now commonly known as the Zamboni, was invented by Frank J. Zamboni in 1949. This invention revolutionized ice maintenance in hockey rinks worldwide.

11. The Stanley Cup's Debut:

The Stanley Cup, the oldest professional sports trophy in North America, was first awarded in 1893. Lord Stanley of Preston, then Governor General of Canada, donated the cup to be presented to Canada's top amateur hockey team.

12. Outdoor Rink Tradition:

The tradition of playing hockey outdoors is deeply rooted. Many Canadians, even today, enjoy playing on frozen ponds, lakes, and backyard rinks during the winter months.

13. Original Six Teams:

In the NHL's early years, there were only six teams known as the "Original Six": Boston Bruins, Chicago Blackhawks, Detroit Red Wings, Montreal Canadiens, New York Rangers, and Toronto Maple Leafs.

14. Hockey Night in Canada:

The iconic "Hockey Night in Canada" broadcast debuted on November 8, 1931. It quickly became a Saturday night tradition for hockey fans across the country.

15. Invention of the Goalie Mask:

Jacques Plante, a Montreal Canadiens goaltender, became the first NHL goalie to regularly wear a mask in 1959. His decision faced resistance initially but soon became standard practice.

16. Fastest Hat Trick:
Bill Mosienko of the Chicago Blackhawks holds the record for the most closed hat trick in NHL history. He scored three goals in 21 seconds on March 23, 1952, against the New York Rangers.

17. The Summit Series:
In 1972, the famous Summit Series occurred between Canada and the Soviet Union. It was a historic eight-game series that ended with a 4-3-1 victory for Canada.

18. NHL Expansion:
The NHL underwent significant expansion in 1967, doubling its size by adding six new teams: Los Angeles Kings, Minnesota North Stars, Philadelphia Flyers, Pittsburgh Penguins, St. Louis Blues, and the California Seals.

19. The Miracle on Ice:
In the 1980 Winter Olympics, the United States hockey team, comprised mainly of college players, achieved the "Miracle on Ice" by defeating the heavily favored Soviet Union team and eventually winning the gold medal.

20. Wayne Gretzky's Records:
Wayne Gretzky, known as "The Great One," holds numerous NHL records, including the most career goals, assists, and points. His impact on the game is immeasurable.

TRIVIA QUIZ 1

1. Origin Quest:
Which Canadian city is often credited as the birthplace of modern ice hockey?

2. Early Stick Material:
What was the traditional material used for early hockey sticks?

3. First Known Country:
Which country has the earliest recorded evidence of people playing ice hockey, dating back to the 19th century?

4. Shinny Slang:
What term is commonly used to describe an informal game of hockey played on outdoor rinks or frozen ponds?

5. European Precursor:

What is the name of the precursor to modern hockey that was played in Europe, particularly in Russia and Scandinavia?

6. English Hockey Variant:

In early English hockey, what did players use instead of a puck?

7. Evolution of the Game:

In the early days of hockey, what did players often use as goals before the modern goalposts?

8. Hockey Stick Transition:

What material replaced wood for making hockey sticks in the evolution of the game?

9. Victorian Era Hockey:

During the Victorian era in England, what term was commonly used for a form of hockey played with a small ball and curved sticks?

10. Hockey in the Olympics:

In which year was ice hockey introduced as an Olympic sport?

11. The First NHL Game:

When was the first official National Hockey League (NHL) game played?

12. Original Six Teams:

Name three out of the Original Six NHL teams?

13. Earliest Hockey Rules:
Who is credited with writing the first known set of rules for the game of hockey?

14. Outdoor Hockey Tradition:
In which Canadian province did the tradition of playing outdoor hockey on frozen ponds become particularly popular?

15. Hockey's Global Spread:
What country outside North America became the first to establish a national hockey association, contributing to the global spread of the sport?

16. Oldest Ice Hockey Trophy:
What is the name of the oldest trophy awarded for professional ice hockey, originally donated by Sir Frederick Arthur Stanley?

17. NHL Team with Most Championships:
Which NHL team holds the record for the most Stanley Cup championships?

18. Hockey Hall of Fame Location:
Where is the Hockey Hall of Fame located in Canada?

19. International Hockey Rivalry:
In international ice hockey, which two countries are known for their intense rivalry, especially in competitions like the Winter Olympics?

20. Women's Hockey Milestone:
When was the first official IIHF Women's World Championship held?

*Answers at the end

JOKE TIME

1. Ice Age Humor:
- Why did the caveman start playing hockey?
- Because he wanted to get his club to the next level!

2. Original Stick Struggles:
- How did early hockey players communicate on the ice?
- With stick signals, but they often got lost in translation!

3. Nordic Nonsense:
- Why did the Viking bring a hockey stick to the battle?
- To score a goal in Valhalla!

4. The Early Zamboni:
- Why did the first hockey games have such smooth ice?
- Because the players kept getting rid of the bumps with their dinosaur skates!

5. Snowman Shenanigans:
- What do snowmen say when playing hockey?
- "Ice to meet you, let's break the ice!"

6. Hockey Time Travel:
- If a time traveler played hockey, which position would they play?
- The goalie, because they're used to stopping history from repeating itself!

JOKE TIME

7. Ancient Arena Antics:
- How did they keep the spectators warm during the first hockey games?
- They had some intense hat-trick bonfires!

8. Pond Hockey Wisdom:
- Why did the pond hockey player bring a ladder to the game?
- To go to the next level of competition!

9. Goalie Giggle:
- Why did the goalie start a comedy club?
- Because he had a great sense of humor, especially when stopping pucks!

10. Early Hockey Chants:
- What did the fans yell during the first hockey games?
- "Freeze the moment, don't let it thaw!"

2. LEGENDS OF THE ICE

- Wayne Gretzky: The Great One
- Bobby Orr: A Defenseman's Dream
- Maurice "Rocket" Richard: Scoring Sensation

WAYNE GRETZKY: THE GREAT ONE

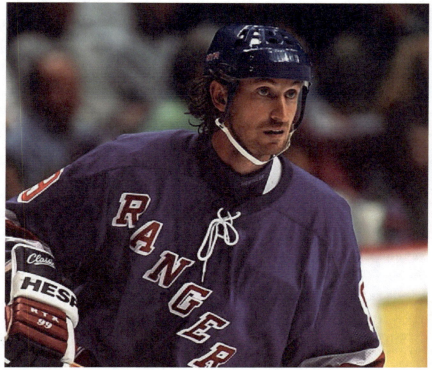

Attribution: By Hakandahlstrom (Håkan Dahlström). IrisKawling uploaded later versions at en. wikipedia. - Originally from en. Wikipedia; description page is/was here. Can also be found at Flickr, CC BY-SA 3.0, https://commons.wikimedia.org/w/index.php?curid=3545164

1.Early Skates:

When he first started skating on double-runner skates, Wayne Gretzky was two years old.

2. Backyard Rink:
Wayne's father, Walter Gretzky, built a backyard rink for his son to practice. This early access to ice proved instrumental in Wayne's development as a hockey player.

3. OHL Phenom:
At just 16 years old, Wayne Gretzky joined the Sault Ste. Marie Greyhounds of the Ontario Hockey League (OHL). He quickly made an impact, scoring 70 goals and 112 assists in his rookie season.

4. Youngest Scorer:
In the 1979-80 NHL season, Wayne Gretzky became the youngest player to score 50 goals in a single season, achieving this feat at 19. He finished the season with 51 goals and 86 assists.

5. High-Scoring Debut:
Wayne Gretzky made his NHL debut with the Edmonton Oilers on October 9, 1979. He marked the occasion with a memorable hat trick, becoming the first player to score three goals in his debut game in 21 years.

6. Record-Breaking Rookie:
Wayne Gretzky's rookie season was nothing short of remarkable. He set 23 different NHL records, including the most points in a season (137), most assists (86), and most goals by a rookie (51).

7. Dynasty Days:
Wayne Gretzky was pivotal in leading the Edmonton Oilers to four Stanley Cup championships in the 1980s (1984, 1985, 1987, and 1988). He was named the Conn Smythe Trophy winner as the most valuable player of the playoffs in 1985 and 1988.

8. The Great Trade:
In one of the most shocking trades in NHL history, Wayne Gretzky was traded from the Edmonton Oilers to the Los Angeles Kings on August 9, 1988. The trade involved 11 players and $15 million in cash.

9. King of Kings:
Despite the trade, Wayne Gretzky continued to excel, becoming the Los Angeles Kings' all-time leading scorer with 285 goals and 590 assists in 583 games. He also led the Kings to their first-ever Stanley Cup Finals appearance in 1993.

10. Kings to Blues:
Wayne Gretzky's NHL career continued with a stint with the St. Louis Blues from 1996 to 1999. He scored 127 goals and 243 assists in 285 games for the Blues.

11. Point-Per-Game Streak:
Wayne Gretzky holds the NHL record for the longest point-per-game streak with 51 consecutive games. During this streak, he scored 61 goals and 77 assists.

12. NHL Awards Magnet:
Wayne Gretzky's dominance on the ice was recognized with a record-breaking nine Hart Memorial Trophies, awarded to the NHL's most valuable player. He also won ten Art Ross Trophies as the league's leading scorer.

13. Coaching Stint:
Following his retirement from playing, Wayne Gretzky took on the role of coach for the Phoenix Coyotes from 2005 to 2009.

14. Business Ventures:
Wayne Gretzky excelled in hockey and business, owning a restaurant, producing wine, and serving as a brand spokesperson.

15. Number 99 Retired:
In 2000, the NHL retired Wayne Gretzky's jersey number 99 league-wide as a tribute to his immense contributions to hockey, making him the only player to receive this honor.

16. Order of Canada:
Wayne Gretzky's impact on Canada was recognized with the Order of Canada, one of the country's highest honors, bestowed upon him in 1984.

17. Olympic Involvement:
During the 2002 Winter Olympics, as the executive director, Wayne Gretzky led Canada's men's hockey team to win the gold medal.

18. A Statue in Edmonton:
Outside Rogers Place in Edmonton stands a bronze statue of Wayne Gretzky, immortalizing his iconic pose.

19. Wayne Gretzky's Restaurant:
Wayne Gretzky's restaurant in Toronto, aptly named "Wayne Gretzky's," offers a unique dining experience featuring hockey memorabilia and interactive games.

20. International Impact:
Wayne Gretzky played for Canada in many international tournaments, including 3 World Championships, 2 Canada Cups, and 2 Winter Olympics. He won gold in 2002 and was an executive director on the team.

21. Scoring Records:

Wayne Gretzky holds numerous NHL records, including most goals (894), most assists (1,963), most points (2,857), most goals in a season (50), most assists in a season (120), most points in a season (215), and most points in a single game (8).

22. Philanthropic Efforts:

Wayne Gretzky supports philanthropic causes, including children's healthcare, education, and cancer research. He founded the Wayne Gretzky Foundation in 2009 to improve the lives of underprivileged children and youth.

BOBBY ORR: A DEFENSEMAN'S DREAM

Attribution: By Aaron Frutman - Flickr: The great Bobby Orr loving it, CC BY 2.0, https://commons.wikimedia.org/w/index.php?curid=24296012

1. Young Phenom: A Rising Star
Bobby Orr made an immediate impact in the NHL when he joined the Boston Bruins at the age of 18. He tallied 13 goals and 28 assists in his rookie season, demonstrating both his offensive potential and defensive prowess.

2. First Norris Trophy: A Remarkable Achievement
Bobby Orr became the youngest player to win the Norris Trophy as the NHL's best defenseman, solidifying his status as a rising star in his second season.

3. Revolutionary Defenseman: Redefining the Role
Bobby Orr transformed the role of defensemen, combining offensive and defensive skills with exceptional skating ability. He was the first defenseman to lead the NHL in scoring, accomplishing this in the 1969-70 season.

4. Stanley Cup Triumph: Leading the Bruins to Victory
Bobby Orr helped lead the Boston Bruins to two Stanley Cup championships in the early 1970s. In the 1970 Stanley Cup Finals, he scored the Cup-winning goal and celebrated by soaring through the air in an iconic moment.

5. Three Straight MVPs: Unparalleled Dominance
Bobby Orr won the Hart Memorial Trophy as the NHL's most valuable player from 1970 to 1972. This unprecedented feat solidified his position as one of the greatest players ever.

6. Orr's Rule: Protecting Goaltenders

The NHL implemented "The Bobby Orr Rule" to prevent goaltenders from handling the puck outside the crease. This rule change was inspired by Orr's offensive maneuvers and aimed to protect goaltenders from collisions.

7. Agent Orr: A Pioneer in Player Representation

Bobby Orr was one of the first NHL players to have a player agent. His decision paved the way for modern player representation, changing the landscape of player contracts and advocating for players' rights.

8. Last Game as a Bruin: A Legendary Career Concluded

Orr's last game as a Bruin was on May 10, 1975, after which he joined the Chicago Blackhawks. During his tenure with the Bruins, he achieved exceptional success, solidifying his status as a franchise icon.

9. Hockey Hall of Fame: A Young Legend

Bobby Orr was inducted into the Hockey Hall of Fame at 31, making him the youngest player ever to receive the honor. This early induction speaks volumes about his impact on the game.

10. Number Retired: Honoring a Legend

The Boston Bruins retired Bobby Orr's No. 4 jersey in 1979 to honor his exceptional contributions, symbolizing his lasting legacy and impact on the team.

11. Post-Hockey Career: A Successful Second Chapter

After retiring, Bobby Orr became a successful player agent. He represented numerous NHL stars and later transitioned into a prominent hockey executive, continuing to contribute to the sport he loved.

12. Statue at TD Garden: A Timeless Celebration

Located outside the TD Garden in Boston, there is a statue of Bobby Orr captured in his famous goal-scoring celebration pose, serving as a constant reminder of his remarkable achievements.

13. Literary Legacy: Sharing His Story

Orr co-authored "Orr: My Story," offering insights into his life, career, triumphs, challenges, and lessons learned.

14. Philanthropy Work: Giving Back to the Community

Bobby Orr is actively involved in various charitable causes, including children's hospitals and organizations dedicated to youth hockey development, reflecting his commitment to making a positive impact

15. Highest-Scoring Defenseman: A Record-Setting Season

Orr set the NHL record for most points by a defenseman in a season with 139 in 1970-71, showcasing his exceptional offensive skills and dominance on the ice.

16. Community Leadership: A Role Model

Orr worked as a special advisor for the Boston Bruins and was actively involved in the community beyond his contributions to the game, demonstrating his leadership and hometown commitment.

17. Bobby Orr Youth Hockey: Inspiring Future Generations
Orr created the Bobby Orr Youth Hockey program to inspire young players, reflecting his passion for the sport and dedication to future generations.

18. Iconic Magazine Cover: A Symbol of Greatness
Orr appeared on the cover of Sports Illustrated 13 times, solidifying his status as a cultural icon and demonstrating his impact on the sports world.

MAURICE "ROCKET" RICHARD: SCORING SENSATION

Attribution: By Conrad Poirier - File:Hockey. Maurice Richard BAnQ P48S1P12157.jpg, Public Domain, https://commons.wikimedia.org/w/index.php?curid=37797587

(1) Original Habs Hero: A Montreal Icon
Maurice Richard, affectionately known as "Rocket" for his explosive speed on the ice, played his entire 18-season NHL career with the Montreal Canadiens, becoming one of the franchise's most revered figures.

(2) Rocket's Debut: A Star Emerges
Richard made his NHL debut with the Canadiens in 1942. He quickly established himself as a formidable player, showcasing exceptional skill and a tireless work ethic. Due to his remarkable ability to accelerate and score seemingly at will, he earned the nickname "Rocket."

(3) First 50-Goal Scorer: A Historic Milestone
During the 1944-45 season, Maurice Richard made history by becoming the first player in NHL to score 50 goals in a single season. This remarkable achievement cemented his position as a scoring sensation. Throughout his career, he continued to display his goal-scoring prowess, leading the league in goals five times.

(4) Habs' Captain: Leading the Charge
Richard served as captain of the Montreal Canadiens from 1956 to 1960, leading his teammates by example with his dedication, passion, and unwavering commitment to winning both on and off the ice.

(5) Hat Trick Record: A Legacy of Excellence
Maurice Richard is the player who holds the record for the most career regular-season hat tricks in Canadiens' history, with an impressive 26. His ability to score multiple goals in a single game further established his reputation as one of the most fearsome offensive threats in the league.

(6) Stanley Cup Glory: A Champion's Role
Throughout his career, Richard played a crucial role in the success of the Montreal Canadiens, helping them win eight Stanley Cups. His contributions were especially notable during the 1955-56 season, when he led the team to a Stanley Cup victory while scoring the most goals in the playoffs.

(7) First Player to Score 500 Goals: A Monumental Achievement
Maurice Richard made history in 1957 as the first player in NHL to score 500 career goals. This was a remarkable achievement that highlighted his exceptional talent and dedication to the game. His success inspired future goal-scorers and cemented his position among the all-time greats of NHL.

(8) Powerful Shot: A Goaltender's Nightmare
Maurice Richard was a constant scoring threat with his powerful and accurate slap shot, feared by opposing goaltenders from any angle.

(9) All-Star Regular: A Star Among Stars
Richard was an exceptional player whose skills and contributions to the game were widely recognized. He was selected to the NHL All-Star Game 13 times during his career, which further solidified his status as one of the league's top players.

(10) Art Ross Trophy Winner: The League's Top Scorer
Richard won the Art Ross Trophy in 1958 as the NHL's leading scorer, solidifying his status as one of the league's top offensive talents.

(11) Richard Riot: A Passionate Fan Base
In 1955, the suspension of Maurice Richard by the NHL sparked widespread protests in Montreal, known as the "Richard Riot." The incident highlighted the deep connection between Richard and the Canadiens' fan base, who passionately defended their beloved player.

(12) Number 9 Retired: A Pioneer of Jersey Retirement
In 1960, the Montreal Canadiens made history by retiring Maurice Richard's No. 9 jersey, becoming the first NHL team to honor a player in this way. This gesture not only solidified Richard's status as a Canadiens legend but also demonstrated his profound impact on the franchise.

(13) Playoff Prowess: A Clutch Performer
Richard's impact on the Canadiens went beyond the regular season. He holds the record for the most game-winning goals in NHL playoff history, showcasing his ability to perform when it mattered the most. His playoff prowess played a vital role in the Canadiens' success.

(14) Hockey Hall of Fame: A Deserved Honor
Maurice Richard was inducted into the Hockey Hall of Fame in 1961, solidifying his place among the sport's greatest legends due to his exceptional talent, unwavering dedication, and impact on the game.

TRIVIA QUIZ 2

Wayne Gretzky: The Great One

1. When did Wayne Gretzky first step onto the NHL ice?

2. What was the traditional material used for early hockey sticks?

3. Which country has the earliest recorded evidence of people playing ice hockey, dating back to the 19th century?

4. What term is commonly used to describe an informal game of hockey played on outdoor rinks or frozen ponds?

5. What is the name of the precursor to modern hockey that was played in Europe, particularly in Russia and Scandinavia?

Bobby Orr: A Defenseman's Dream

6. Before donning the Chicago Blackhawks jersey, Bobby Orr was a defensive force for which NHL team?

7. What enduring image is linked to Bobby Orr's unforgettable Stanley Cup-winning goal in 1970?

8. During his illustrious career, how many Norris Trophies did Bobby Orr claim as the NHL's best defenseman?

9. "The Bobby Orr Rule" aimed to prevent goaltenders from what action?

10. Which jersey number did the Boston Bruins retire in tribute to Bobby Orr?

Maurice "Rocket" Richard: Scoring Sensation

11, What was the electrifying nickname bestowed upon Maurice Richard?

12. In which hockey season did Maurice Richard become the trailblazer, scoring an unprecedented 50 goals?

13. How many times did Maurice Richard hoist the Stanley Cup with the Montreal Canadiens?

14. The "Richard Riot" erupted in 1955 following his suspension by the NHL. What led to this controversial decision?

15. The Montreal Canadiens retired which jersey number to immortalize Maurice Richard?

JOKE TIME

1. The Great One's Autograph:
- Why did the puck ask Wayne Gretzky for his autograph?
- Because it wanted to be signed by "The Great One" too!

2. Bobby Orr's GPS:
- Why did Bobby Orr get lost on the way to the hockey rink?
- His GPS kept telling him to take a flying leap!

3. Rocket's High Score:
- How did Maurice Richard score so many goals?
- He had a "rocket" shot that always reached the net!

4. Bench Chat:
- Why don't hockey players ever sit next to the computer during the game?
- Because they might get a byte from the Sharks!

5. Gretzky's Bedtime:
- Why did Wayne Gretzky sleep with his hockey stick?
- In case he had a nightmare about a breakaway!
-

6. Orr's Shopping Trip:
- Why did Bobby Orr go to the grocery store after a game?
- He heard they had a great deal on "slap-chops"!

Joke Time

7. Richard's Comedy Night:
- Why did Maurice Richard become a stand-up comedian after retiring?
- He knew how to deliver a punchline on and off the ice!

8. Locker Room Riddle:
- Why did the hockey player bring a ladder to the locker room?
- To go to the next level of competition!

9. The Three Legends' Coffee Shop:
- Wayne Gretzky, Bobby Orr, and Maurice Richard walk into a coffee shop.
- The barista asks, "How do you take your coffee?"
- They all respond, "With a Stanley Cup, please!"

10. Goalie's Wisdom:
- Why did the goalie become a philosopher?
- Because he knew how to save deep thoughts!

3. STANLEY CUP GLORY

- The Quest for Lord Stanley's Cup
- Historic Stanley Cup Moments
- Canadian Dominance in the NHL

THE QUEST FOR LORD STANLEY'S CUP

1. **Lord Stanley's Donation:**
   - In 1892, the Governor General of Canada, Sir Frederick Arthur Stanley, donated the Stanley Cup trophy.

2. **Original Design:**
   - The original Stanley Cup had a bowl-like shape, but it has since evolved into the iconic design we see today.

3. **Championship Tradition:**
   - The Stanley Cup is the oldest trophy awarded in professional sports. It has a rich tradition of engraving winning teams and players.

4. **Traveling Cup:**
   - The Stanley Cup has been used as a flower pot and left at the roadside, among other unique locations.

5. **The Keeper of the Cup:**
   - The person responsible for the Cup is known as the "Keeper of the Cup," and they accompany it wherever it goes.

6. **Multiple Trophies:**
   - The Stanley Cup predates the NHL and was contested by multiple leagues. It became the NHL's top prize in 1926.

7. **Cup Controversies:**
   - Over the years, there have been amusing and unusual stories surrounding the Stanley Cup. It has been thrown into a canal and used for baptisms.

8. Day with the Cup:
- Each player on the championship-winning team gets to spend a day with the Stanley Cup, creating memorable moments and traditions.

9. Miniature Versions:
- The NHL presents each player and staff member of the winning team with a miniature version of the Stanley Cup called the "Stanley Cup Ring."

10. Stanley Cup Trust:
- The Stanley Cup Trust ensures that the trophy is kept in top condition and that its rich history is preserved for future generations.

Attribution: By Michael Righi - originally posted to Flickr as Pavel Datsyuk, CC BY-SA 2.0, https://commons.wikimedia.org/w/index.php?curid=4185459

HISTORIC STANLEY CUP MOMENTS

1. Longest Game:
- The longest game in Stanley Cup Finals history occurred in 1936 when the Detroit Red Wings and Montreal Maroons played for six overtimes.

2. Fastest Hat Trick:
- Bill Mosienko scored the fastest hat trick in Stanley Cup history, netting three goals in just 21 seconds during a 1952 game.

3. Original Six Dominance:
- The Montreal Canadiens, Toronto Maple Leafs, and Detroit Red Wings dominated the Cup during the Original Six era (1942-1967).

4. Gretzky's Point Record:
- Wayne Gretzky set the record for most points in a single Stanley Cup Finals series, scoring 13 points in 1985.

5. Overtime Magic:
- Jacques Plante was the first goalie to record a shutout in a Stanley Cup Finals overtime game, achieving this feat in 1953.

6. Hat Trick of Hat Tricks:
- Wayne Gretzky accomplished a rare feat in 1981 by scoring a hat trick in each period of a playoff game.

7. Youngest Captain's Triumph:
- Sidney Crosby led the Pittsburgh Penguins to win the Stanley Cup in 2009, becoming the youngest captain to do so.

8. Five Goals in a Game:
- Newsy Lalonde was the first player to score five goals in a single Stanley Cup game, achieving this feat in 1919.

9. Unbelievable Comebacks:
- The Toronto Maple Leafs and the New York Islanders share the record for the largest comeback in a Stanley Cup series, both overcoming 3-0 deficits.

10. Brotherly Love:
- The Sutter family holds a unique distinction in the NHL, with six brothers having played and several winning the Stanley Cup during their careers.

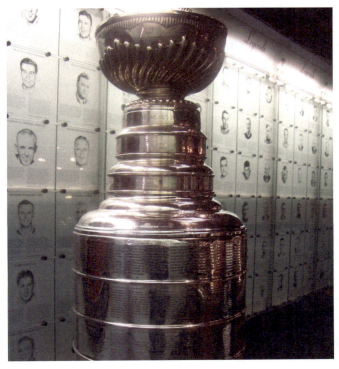

By Own work, Public Domain, https://commons.wikimedia.org/w/index.php?curid=1390419

CANADIAN DOMINANCE IN THE NHL

1. **Original Six Era:**
   - The Original Six era featured Canadian teams such as the Montreal Canadiens, Toronto Maple Leafs, and Detroit Red Wings. It was a period of Canadian hockey dominance.

2. **Dynasty of the Oilers:**
   - The Edmonton Oilers, led by Wayne Gretzky, dominated the NHL in the 1980s and won multiple Stanley Cups.

3. **Montreal's Golden Era:**
   - The Montreal Canadiens have won the most Stanley Cups in NHL history, with 24 championships.

4. **The Canadian Triple Crown:**
   - The Montreal Canadiens won the Stanley Cup, the Prince of Wales Trophy, and the Art Ross Trophy in the 1976-77 season.

5. **The Great One's Influence:**
   - Wayne Gretzky's impact on Canadian hockey is immeasurable, contributing to the growth and popularity of the sport in the country.

6. **Goaltending Legends:**
   - Canada has produced many legendary goaltenders who have left an indelible mark on the NHL, including Patrick Roy, Martin Brodeur, and Terry Sawchuk.

7. **Hall of Famers Galore:**
   - Canada has a rich hockey history, with many players in the Hockey Hall of Fame.

8. Olympic Triumphs:
- Canada has consistently dominated international competitions, including various Olympic tournaments.

9. Great Canadian Rivalries:
- Intense rivalries between Canadian teams, such as the Battle of Alberta (Calgary Flames vs. Edmonton Oilers), add excitement to the NHL season.

10. Maple Leafs' Glory Days:
- The Toronto Maple Leafs won four Stanley Cups in six years during their dominant period in the 1960s, contributing to their storied history.

The Quest for Lord Stanley's Cup

1. Who donated the original Stanley Cup in 1892?

2. What was the original shape of the Stanley Cup when it was first donated?

3. In what year did the Stanley Cup become the premier prize of the NHL?

4. What is the official title of the person responsible for the Stanley Cup's care?

5. Which Canadian Governor General was responsible for donating the trophy that became the Stanley Cup?

6. What is the tradition associated with the Stanley Cup's engraving?

7. In the early years, which leagues competed for the Stanley Cup before it became the NHL's premier prize?

8. What unique locations has the Stanley Cup visited over the years?

9. What is the miniature version of the Stanley Cup presented to players and staff members?

10. What organization ensures the preservation of the Stanley Cup's rich history?

Historic Stanley Cup Moments

1. In what year did the longest Stanley Cup Finals game take place, lasting six overtime?

2. Who holds the record for the fastest hat trick in Stanley Cup history?

3. During which era did the Original Six teams dominate the Stanley Cup?

4. Who holds the record for the most points in a single Stanley Cup Finals series, tallying 13 points in 1985?

5. In 1953, who became the first goalie to record a shutout in a Stanley Cup Finals overtime game?

6. Which player achieved the rare feat of scoring a hat trick in every period of a playoff game in 1981?

7. Who became the youngest captain to win the Stanley Cup, leading the Pittsburgh Penguins in 2009?

8. Who scored five goals in a single Stanley Cup game in 1919?

9. Which teams share the record for the largest comeback in a Stanley Cup series, overcoming 3-0 deficits?

10. How many brothers from the Sutter family played in the NHL, with several winning the Stanley Cup?

Canadian Dominance in the NHL

1. During which era did the Original Six teams dominate the NöHL, featuring Canadian teams like the Montreal Canadiens and Toronto Maple Leafs?

2. Which team, led by Wayne Gretzky, dominated the NHL in the 1980s, winning multiple Stanley Cups?

3. How many Stanley Cups have the Montreal Canadiens won, making them the team with the most championships in NHL history?

4. What did the Montreal Canadiens achieve in the 1976-77 season, winning the Stanley Cup, the Prince of Wales Trophy, and the Art Ross Trophy?

5. What impact did Wayne Gretzky have on Canadian hockey, contributing to the growth and popularity of the sport?

6. Name three legendary Canadian goaltenders who have left an indelible mark on the NHL.

7. How many players from Canada are in the Hockey Hall of Fame?

8. Which Canadian team won four Stanley Cups in six years during the 1960s?

9. Which intense rivalry between Canadian teams adds excitement to the NHL season?

10. In the 1980s, which Canadian team, led by Wayne Gretzky, dominated the NHL in a dynasty-like fashion?

Joke Time

(a) The Quest for Lord Stanley's Cup

1. Keeper of the Cup:
- Why did the Keeper of the Cup become a stand-up comedian?
- Because he had a trophy case full of jokes!

2. Traveling Troubles:
- Why did the Stanley Cup refuse to travel abroad?
- It didn't want to get caught up in international hockey relations!

3. Engraving Euphoria:
- Why did the engraver bring a ladder to work on the Stanley Cup?
- To reach new heights in trophy engraving!

4. Cup Confessions:
- What did the Stanley Cup say to the other trophies?
- "I've been around the rink a few times!"

Joke Time

(b) Historic Stanley Cup Moments

5. Overtime Odyssey:
- Why did the hockey player bring a pillow to the game?
- In case he needed to catch some shut-eye during a long overtime!

6. Hat Trick Havoc:
- How did the hat feel after being thrown onto the ice for the third time?
- It was on top of the world!

7. Original Six Stand-Up:
- Why did the comedian only tell jokes about the Original Six teams?
- Because the classics never go out of style!

8. Record Breaker:
- Why did the hockey player bring a camera to the game?
- To capture the moment when he broke a record!

JOKE TIME

(c) Canadian Dominance in the NHL

9. Maple Leaf Mix-Up:
- Why did the Maple Leafs go to the hockey game?
- It wanted to be part of a Leafs victory!

10. Wayne's World:
- Why did Wayne Gretzky start a garden?
- Because he wanted to grow the Great One's Tana!

4. THE HEROES' JOURNEYS

- Kid Heroes of the NHL
- Rookie Sensations
- Young Players Who Captured Hearts

KID HEROES OF THE NHL

1. Sidney Crosby's Early Start:
- Sidney Crosby, one of the biggest stars in the NHL, began playing hockey at three in his hometown of Cole Harbour, Nova Scotia.

2. Connor McDavid's Exceptional Skills:
- Connor McDavid, nicknamed "The Next One," began playing organized hockey at age four and was reading at a third-grade level in kindergarten.

3. Matthews' International Journey:
- Auston Matthews was born in San Ramon, California. He was the first player from Arizona to be selected first overall in the NHL Draft.

4. Ovechkin's Young Achievements:
- Alexander Ovechkin scored his first goal at age ten, after playing his first organized game at age eight. He is known for his powerful scoring.

5. Marner's Early Promise:
- Mitch Marner, a dynamic forward for the Toronto Maple Leafs, was drafted fourth overall in 2015 after an impressive junior career with the London Knights.

6. Dahlin's Historic Entry:
- Rasmus Dahlin, a Swedish defenseman, was selected first overall in the 2018 NHL Draft, making him the highest-drafted Swede in history.

7. Barzal's Junior Success:
- Mathew Barzal, a key player for the New York Islanders, won the WHL Player of the Year award during his junior career with the Seattle Thunderbirds.

8. Hughes Brothers' Impact:
- Jack and Quinn Hughes, two talented brothers, were both selected in the first round of the NHL Draft, showcasing their family's hockey skills.

9. Kaprizov's KHL Experience:
- Kirill Kaprizov, a Russian forward, played in the Kontinental Hockey League (KHL) before significantly impacting the NHL with the Minnesota Wild.

10. Pettersson's Calder Trophy:
- Elias Pettersson, a talented forward for the Vancouver Canucks, was awarded the Calder Trophy as the NHL's Rookie of the Year for the 2018-19 season.

Evgeni Malkin

By Michael Miller - Own work, CC BY-SA 4.0, https://commons.wikimedia.org/w/index.php?curid=76195294

ROOKIE SENSATIONS

1. The Legend of Gretzky's Rookie Year:
- Wayne Gretzky amassed an incredible 137 points during his rookie season in the NHL in 1979-80, setting the stage for his legendary career.

2. Orr's Unprecedented Wins:
- Bobby Orr, a defensive sensation, won the Calder Trophy as the NHL's Rookie of the Year in 1967 and revolutionized the role of defensemen.

3. Crosby's Immediate Impact:
- Sidney Crosby showcased his talent by scoring 102 points in his rookie season with the Pittsburgh Penguins after joining the league in 2005.

4. Brodeur's Goaltending Prowess:
- Martin Brodeur had a remarkable rookie season in 1993-94, setting the stage for his legendary career with the New Jersey Devils as one of the greatest goaltenders of all time.

5. Kane's Calder Trophy Win:
- Patrick Kane won the Calder Trophy in 2008 for his outstanding rookie season with the Chicago Blackhawks as a dynamic forward.

6. Eichel's Entry into Buffalo:
- Jack Eichel, who was drafted second overall in 2015, immediately made an impact as a rookie with the Buffalo Sabres by showcasing his scoring prowess.

7. Lafleur's Dazzling Start:
- Guy Lafleur, a Montreal Canadiens legend, scored 29 goals in his rookie year during the 1971-72 season.

8. The Rise of Teemu Selanne:
- Teemu Selanne, a Finnish forward, set a rookie record with 76 goals in the 1992-93 season, which still stands today.

9. Crosby vs. Ovechkin:
- The 2005-06 NHL season saw the beginning of a rivalry that would define the next era of hockey between Sidney Crosby and Alexander Ovechkin.

10. Connor McDavid's Arrival:
- Connor McDavid, who was selected first overall in 2015, displayed his speed and skill as a rookie, setting high expectations for his future with the Edmonton Oilers.

Auston Matthews

By Quintin Soloviev - Own work, CC BY-SA 4.0, https://commons.wikimedia.org/w/index.php?curid=124520861

YOUNG PLAYERS WHO CAPTURED HEARTS

1. Bure's Explosive Entry:
- Pavel Bure, a Russian hockey player, earned the nickname "The Russian Rocket" after his impressive rookie season with the Vancouver Canucks in 1991-92.

2. Lemieux's Early Brilliance:
- A hockey legend, Mario Lemieux scored 100 points in his rookie season with the Pittsburgh Penguins in 1984-85, foreshadowing his Hall of Fame career.

3. Gretzky's Prolific Start:
- Wayne Gretzky's early years with the Edmonton Oilers saw him capture the hearts of fans with his incredible scoring and playmaking abilities.

4. The Sedins' Twin Magic:
- Daniel and Henrik Sedin, twin brothers from Sweden, played their entire careers with the Vancouver Canucks, captivating fans with their telepathic connection on the ice.

5. Joe Thornton's Impact:
- Joe Thornton, known for his incredible playmaking, immediately made an impact in the NHL with the Boston Bruins. He captured the hearts of fans with his skill.

6. Lafontaine's All-Star Start:
- Pat Lafontaine, a dynamic forward, earned an All-Star appearance in his rookie season with the New York Islanders in 1984-85.

7. Hasek's Goaltending Brilliance:

- Dominik Hasek, a legendary goaltender, started his NHL career with the Chicago Blackhawks. He quickly won over fans with his acrobatic saves.

8. Stamkos' Lightning Speed:

- Steven Stamkos quickly became a fan favorite with the Tampa Bay Lightning due to his prolific goal-scoring ability.

9. Datsyuk's Magic Touch:

- Pavel Datsyuk, a Russian hockey player known for his stickhandling and defensive skills, quickly became a fan favorite upon joining the Detroit Red Wings.

10. Malkin's Arrival in Pittsburgh:

- Evgeni Malkin was selected second overall in the 2004 NHL draft. In his rookie season with the Pittsburgh Penguins, he formed a dynamic duo with Sidney Crosby and made a significant impact.

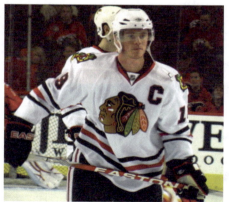

Jonathan Toews

By Resolute - Own work, CC BY-SA 3.0, https://commons.wikimedia.org/w/index.php?curid=6598409

Kid Heroes of the NHL

1. At what age did Sidney Crosby start playing hockey?

2. Who is known as "The Next One" and read at a third-grade level in kindergarten?

3. Where was Auston Matthews born before becoming the first overall pick in the NHL Draft?

4. At what age did Alexander Ovechkin play his first organized hockey game?

5. Which player won the WHL Player of the Year award during his junior career with the Seattle Thunderbirds?

Rookie Sensations

6. In what season did Wayne Gretzky amass 137 points in his rookie year?

7. Who won the Calder Trophy as the NHL's Rookie of the Year in 1967 and revolutionized the role of defensemen?

8. What was the record set by Teemu Selanne as a rookie in the 1992-93 season?

9. How many points did Sidney Crosby score in his rookie season with the Pittsburgh Penguins?

10. Who won the Calder Trophy in 2008 after a stellar rookie season with the Chicago Blackhawks?

Rookie Sensations

11. What nickname was given to Pavel Bure during his rookie season with the Vancouver Canucks?

12. Who recorded 29 goals in his rookie year with the Montreal Canadiens in the 1971-72 season?

13. In which season did Wayne Gretzky capture the hearts of fans with his incredible scoring and playmaking abilities?

14. How many points did Joe Thornton earn in his rookie season with the Boston Bruins in 1997-98?

15. Who are the twin brothers from Sweden who played their entire careers with the Vancouver Canucks?

JOKE TIME

(a) Kid Heroes of the NHL

1. **Early Starter:**
   - Why did the little hockey player bring a ladder to practice?
   - To reach the top shelf of the trophy case early!
2. **Sidney's Snack:**
   - What's Sidney Crosby's favorite subject in school?
   - History, because he loves adding chapters to his own!
3. **McDavid's Homework:**
   - Why did Connor McDavid finish his homework so quickly?
   - Because he knows how to accelerate!
4. **Auston's California Dreamin':**
   - Why did Auston Matthews bring sunscreen to the hockey game?
   - He's used to the California sun!
5. **Ovechkin's Playground:**
   - What was Alexander Ovechkin's favorite game as a kid?
   - Duck, Duck, Snipe!

JOKE TIME

(b) Rookie Sensations

1. Gretzky's GPS:
- Why did Wayne Gretzky make a great navigator?
- Because he always knew the best way to the net!

2. Orr's Defense Mechanism:
- Why did Bobby Orr become a comedian after retiring?
- He knew the best way to deflect attention!

3. Kane's Coin Toss:
- How does Patrick Kane make decisions?
- He flips a puck instead of a coin!

4. Crosby's Grocery List:
- What's on Sidney Crosby's grocery list?
- Bread, milk, eggs, and a dozen goals!

JOKE TIME

(c) Young Players Who Captured Hearts

1. Heartthrob Hockey:
- Why did the hockey player bring a hammer to the game?
- To break the ice and steal some hearts!

2. Sedins' Secret Code:
- Why do Daniel and Henrik Sedin never need to speak on the ice?
- They have a twin-telepathic connection!

3. Jagr's Fountain of Youth:
- How does Jaromir Jagr stay so young in hockey?
- He found the Fountain of Youth... somewhere between the blue line and the net!

5. PUCK DREAMS ON CANADIAN SOIL

- Backyard Rinks and Frozen Ponds
- Learning to Skate and Shoot
- From Pick-Up Games to Organized Hockey

BACKYARD RINKS AND FROZEN PONDS

1. Community Tradition:
- Many Canadian communities host competitions for the best backyard rink, transforming winter into a friendly and creative contest of skill.

2. Ephemeral Artistry:
- Instead of just being used for hockey, some families turn backyard rinks into temporary works of art by creating intricate designs and patterns on the frozen canvas.

3. Nighttime Magic:
- Backyard rinks often come alive at night with the glow of strategically placed lights, turning the ordinary into a magical winter wonderland.

4. DIY Innovations:
- Canadians are known for their DIY spirit. Some backyard rinks feature ingenious additions like homemade scoreboards, player benches, and even mini Zambonis.

5. Neighborhood Showdowns:
- Friendly neighborhood games on backyard rinks create unforgettable memories for players and spectators and strengthen community bonds.

6. Winter Wildlife Visitors:
- Frozen ponds and backyard rinks attract wildlife in winter, bringing nature to the hockey experience with occasional visits from curious animals.

7. Family Hockey Night:
- Family hockey nights on backyard rinks create a multi-generational love for the sport.

8. Tournament Atmosphere:
- Some families hold backyard ice hockey tournaments with brackets and trophies.

9. Therapeutic Ice Time:
- Skating on a backyard rink under the open sky is not just a sport; it's a therapeutic activity allowing Canadians to embrace winter's beauty.

10. Winter Social Hub:
- Backyard rinks are social hubs where friends and family gather for winter activities, hot chocolate, and bonfires.

Bobby Orr

LEARNING TO SKATE AND SHOOT

1. First Skate Memories:
- Many NHL players fondly recall their first experiences on skates, emphasizing the importance of learning to balance and glide before picking up a stick.

2. Frozen Artistry:
- Kids often turn their snow-covered driveways into makeshift hockey rinks, practicing their shots and dreaming of scoring the winning goal.

3. Parental Coaches:
- Parents in Canada often become skilled coaches, passing on their love for skating and shooting to their children.

4. Snowbank Challenges:
- Snowbanks are transformed into natural barriers for practicing stickhandling skills. Players weave through the obstacles to enhance their agility.

5. Frozen Pond Symphonies:
- Shooting on frozen ponds creates a rhythmic soundtrack as pucks slap against the ice, a symphony of sounds synonymous with winter.

6. Shovel and Shoot:
- While shoveling the driveway, players seize the opportunity to hone their shooting accuracy and power.

Mario Lemieux

Attribution: By Tony McCune - Flickr: Mario Lemieux, Hall of Famer, CC BY 2.0, https://commons.wikimedia.org/w/index.php?curid=30300081

7. Winter Olympics at Home:
- Kids often imitate their favorite Winter Olympic events on ice-covered driveways, combining their love for hockey with imaginative competitions.

8. Mini Stick Tournaments:
- Mini-stick tournaments held in basements and garages often spark a passion for the game and friendly sibling rivalries.

9. Skating Races:
- Learning to skate involves friendly races on frozen ponds, where friends and siblings compete to see who is the fastest skater in the neighborhood.

10. Snowy Saucer Passes:
- Snowy surfaces are perfect for practicing saucer passes, allowing players to perfect sending the puck smoothly to their teammates.

FROM PICK-UP GAMES TO ORGANIZED HOCKEY

1. First Pick-Up Game Magic:
- The magic of the first pickup game often happens on frozen ponds, with players embracing the freedom of unstructured play and spontaneous competition.

2. Organized Hockey Dreams:
- Playing organized hockey is a dream come true for many young Canadians, symbolizing the transition from casual games to more structured competition.

3. Winter Roadside Arenas:
- During winter, some communities create hockey rinks on frozen lakes, complete with boards, resulting in picturesque scenes.

4. Vintage Hockey Gear Treasures:
- The transition to organized hockey usually involves purchasing official gear. However, many Canadians have fond memories of using vintage equipment handed down from family members.

5. Community Hockey Heroes:
- Organized hockey introduces young players to local community heroes such as coaches, veteran players, and volunteers who contribute to the love of the game.

6. Winter Carnival Classics:
- Winter carnivals often include pickup games as a staple, where participants can showcase their skills at the heart of community celebrations.

7. Hockey Mom MVPs:
- Hockey moms play a central role, providing unwavering support, washing countless jerseys, and cheering from the stands during both pick-up games and organized leagues.

8. Team Names and Legends:
- Pick-up games involve players creating quirky team names and legends, adding fun to unstructured play.

9. Friendly Neighborhood Showdowns:
- During winter, neighborhoods turn into lively outdoor arenas with pick-up games, laughter, and excitement.

10. Outdoor Rink Chronicles:
- The transition to organized hockey often involves sharing stories of favorite outdoor rinks. Each player has cherished memories of community ice.

Joe Sakic
By Hakandahlstrom at English Wikipedia, CC BY-SA 3.0,
https://commons.wikimedia.org/w/index.php?curid=9927609

TRIVIA QUIZ 5

Backyard Rinks and Frozen Ponds

1. What annual competitions do many Canadian communities hold related to backyard rinks?

2. What transforms backyard rinks into temporary works of art?

3. What do some families add to their backyard rinks for maintenance, resembling a makeshift Zamboni?

4. Besides hockey, what else do frozen ponds attract on occasion?

5. What turns backyard rinks into social hubs?

Learning to Skate and Shoot

1. What becomes a temporary shooting gallery for aspiring young players?

2. What do parents often become when teaching their kids to skate and shoot?

3. What do kids often use as natural barriers for practicing stickhandling skills?efensemen?

4. What becomes an impromptu rhythmic soundtrack when learning to shoot on frozen ponds?

5. Besides shooting, what is shoveling the driveway an opportunity for?

From Pick-Up Games to Organized Hockey

1 Where does the magic of the first pick-up game often happen for many young Canadians?

2. What does playing organized hockey symbolize for many young players?

3. What do some communities transform into makeshift arenas for pick-up games?

4. What often happens during winter carnivals in terms of hockey?

5. Who takes center stage in organized hockey, providing support and cheering from the stands?

JOKE TIME

Backyard Rinks and Frozen Ponds

1. Why did the snowman apply to play on the backyard hockey team?
He heard they needed a good "slapshot" artist!

2: What do you call a snowbank on a Canadian driveway?
The perfect natural obstacle for a future NHL stickhandling pro!

3. Why did the hockey puck bring a shovel to the backyard rink?
To clean up its "ice-olated" mess!

4. How do Canadian ducks spend their winter days?
Enjoying a game of "duck, duck, skate" on frozen ponds!

5. Why did the Zamboni start telling jokes during its rounds on the backyard rink?
To break the ice, of course!

JOKE TIME

Learning to Skate and Shoot

1. **Why was the hockey player a great comedian on the ice?**
   - Because he had a "puck"-ish sense of humor!

2. **What did the stick say to the puck during their practice session?**
   - "Let's stick together and glide through this, buddy!"

3. **How do you make a hockey player laugh on the ice?**
   - Tell them a "cool" joke and watch them crack up while trying to keep their balance!

4. **Why did the young hockey player bring a ladder to the rink?**
   - To take their skills to the next level!

5. **What do you call a snowman who's an expert at hockey?**
   - A "slap-frost" champion!

JOKE TIME

From Pick-Up Games to Organized Hockey

1. Why did the hockey player bring a broom to the pick-up game?
   - To sweep the competition, of course!

2. How do hockey players stay cool during a heated pick-up game?
   - They stand near the fans!

3. Why was the pick-up hockey game like a story?
   - Because every game had its own "plot" twist!

4. What's a hockey player's favorite kind of music during a pick-up game?
   - Anything with a good "beat"!

5. Why do pick-up games in Canada always have great attendance?
   - Because the players never miss a chance to "stick" together!

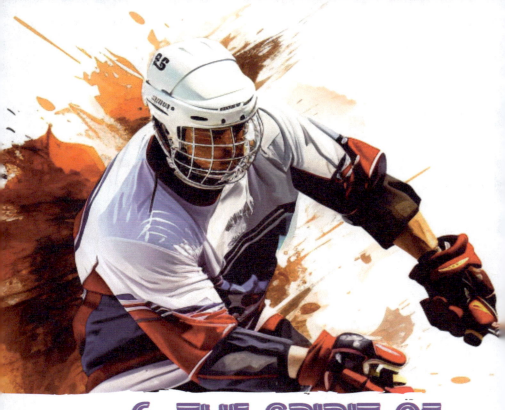

6. THE SPIRIT OF CANADIAN HOCKEY

- Values and Traditions of the Game
- Sportsmanship and Teamwork
- The Role of Coaches and Mentors

VALUES AND TRADITIONS OF THE GAME

1. The Hockey Sweater:
- Many young Canadians can relate to the iconic story of "The Hockey Sweater" by Roch Carrier, illustrating the deep cultural connection between hockey and Canadian identity.

2. The Molson Cup:
- The Molson Cup, which is awarded to the most valuable player of the Montreal Canadiens, has a rich history and represents excellence in the NHL.

3. Original Six Rivalries:
- The intense rivalries among the Original Six NHL teams - the Montreal Canadiens, Toronto Maple Leafs, Boston Bruins, Chicago Blackhawks, Detroit Red Wings, and New York Rangers - are deeply rooted in Canadian hockey history.

4. Heritage Classic:
- The NHL's Heritage Classic is an outdoor game that celebrates the sport's roots, often played in iconic Canadian settings, like Regina's tundra or Edmonton's snowy landscapes.

5. Hockey Night in Canada:
- "Hockey Night in Canada" is a beloved Canadian tradition that brings families together every Saturday to watch the national pastime and enjoy the iconic theme music.

6. Good Luck Charm:
- Many hockey players have superstitions, such as not shaving during winning streaks or following specific rituals before games. These traditions contribute to the rich tapestry of hockey culture.

7. Stanley Cup Beards:

- Growing a playoff beard is a tradition among players during the quest for the Stanley Cup. It signifies unity and commitment.

8. Three Stars of the Game:

- After each match, fans eagerly await the announcement of the three stars of the game, a tradition that highlights outstanding player performances.

9. Overtime Playoff Intensity:

- Playoff overtime in hockey is a thrilling tradition where sudden-death goals can occur at any moment, elevating the intensity and drama of the sport.

Gordie Howe
Attribution:By Ralston-Purina Company, makers of Chex cereals - eBayfrontback, Public Domain, https://commons.wikimedia.org/w/index.php?curid=31185471

SPORTSMANSHIP AND TEAMWORK

1. The Hockey Handshake:
- The tradition of post-game handshakes in hockey emphasizes sportsmanship and respect for opponents.

2. Captain Leadership:
- Ice hockey team captains play a vital role as they lead their team on and off the ice, using their skills, charisma, and sportsmanship.

3. Hat Tricks for Charity:
- Some players donate to charity for every hat trick they score, turning achievements into opportunities to give back to the community.

4. Team Prayer Rituals:
- Some teams have pre-game or post-game prayer rituals, emphasizing unity, respect, and a sense of purpose beyond the game.

5. Stick Taps:
- Players often tap their sticks on the ice to acknowledge good plays, goals, or critical moments, showcasing camaraderie and mutual respect.

6. Jersey Swaps:
- The tradition of players exchanging jerseys after a game is a symbol of mutual respect and a display of the global fraternity of hockey players.

7. Community Outreach:
- Many hockey teams engage in community outreach to support local charities, schools, and youth programs.

8. The Selke Trophy:
- The Frank J. Selke Trophy is awarded to the forward who best excels in the defensive aspects of the game, highlighting the importance of a well-rounded approach and teamwork.

9. Team Celebrations:
- Team celebrations, from coordinated goal celebrations to post-victory rituals, create bonds between players and entertain fans.

10. Captain's Handshake with Officials:
- The pre-game tradition of team captains shaking hands with officials symbolizes mutual respect between players and those maintaining fair play.

Jean Béliveau

Attribution:By Ralrton-Purina Company, maker of Chex cereals - eBayfrontback, Public Domain, https://commons.wikimedia.org/w/index.php?curid=65116734

THE ROLE OF COACHES AND MENTORS

1. Scotty Bowman's Legacy:
- Scotty Bowman, with his record-breaking coaching career and numerous Stanley Cup victories, is a legendary figure whose influence extends beyond coaching to mentorship.

2. Pat Quinn's Leadership:
- Pat Quinn was an impactful leader as both a player and a coach, emphasizing balance between discipline, strategy, and camaraderie.

3. The Art of Coaching:
- Coaches play a crucial role in developing players as athletes and individuals, imparting life skills and values that extend beyond the rink.

4. Behind-the-Bench Rituals:
- Coaches often have pre-game rituals, such as wearing lucky suits or giving motivating speeches. These superstitions add to their strategic roles.

5. Coaching Mentorship Programs:
- Mentorship programs are common for aspiring coaches, where experienced mentors pass down their wisdom and techniques to the next generation.

6. The Jack Adams Award:
- The Jack Adams Award is presented to the NHL's top coach in recognition of their impact on team success and player development.

7. Legacy of Herb Brooks:
- Herb Brooks' coaching legacy, especially his involvement in the 1980 U.S. Olympic team's "Miracle on Ice," inspires coaches and players.

8. In-Game Strategy:
- Coaches showcase the complexity of coaching by strategically matching lines, designing plays, and making split-second decisions during games, much like a game of chess.

9. Player-Coach Relationships:
- Successful coaches establish strong player relationships, identifying strengths, motivating, and building trust.

10. Coaching Tree Connections:
- The coaching tree highlights the enduring influence of mentorship in hockey as successful coaches produce proteges who go on to become successful coaches themselves.

Clare Drake

Values and Traditions of the Game

1. What iconic Canadian story by Roch Carrier emphasizes the deep connection between hockey and Canadian identity?

2. Which trophy is awarded to the Montreal Canadiens' most valuable player and is a symbol of excellence in the NHL?

3. Name three teams among the Original Six in the NHL.

4. What is a cherished Canadian tradition that brings families together every Saturday to watch hockey?

5. What is the Heritage Classic, and where is it often played?

Sportsmanship and Teamwork

1. What is the post-game tradition in hockey that emphasizes sportsmanship and respect for opponents?

2. Who holds a special role in hockey, serving as a leader on and off the ice?

3. What do some players pledge to do for charity when they score a hat trick?

4. What is a common gesture of mutual admiration and a display of the global fraternity of hockey players?

5. What do players often do to acknowledge good plays, goals, or important moments during a game?

The Role of Coaches and Mentors

1 Who is considered a legendary figure in coaching with a record-breaking career and numerous Stanley Cup victories?

2. Who was an influential figure both as a player and a coach, emphasizing a balance between discipline, strategy, and camaraderie?

3. What is the award given to the best coach in the NHL?

4. Whose legacy is associated with the "Miracle on Ice" with the 1980 U.S. Olympic team?

5. What does the term "coaching tree connections" refer to in hockey?

JOKE TIME

Values and Traditions of the Game

1. Why did the hockey player bring a pen to the game?
   - To draw a "line" in the ice for fair play!

2. What did the hockey puck say to the net?
   - "You're a goal-oriented individual!"

3. Why do hockey players make excellent musicians?
   - Because they have great "slap" skills!

4. How do hockey players stay cool during a game?
   - They stand near the fans!

5. Why did the hockey coach go to the bank?
   - To get his goalie!

Sportsmanship and Teamwork

6. What do you call a friendly hockey match between animals?
   - A "polar bear" hug!

7. How do hockey players keep in touch with each other?
   - They "stick" together!

8. What did the hockey player say to the goalie on their birthday?
   - "I hope your day is a 'net' gain!"

JOKE TIME

9. Why did the hockey player bring a ladder to the game?
- To take their skills to the next level!

10. What did the hockey stick say to the puck?
- "You make my heart 'slapshot'!"

The Role of Coaches and Mentors

11. Why did the coach bring a ladder to practice?
- To help the team reach new heights!

12. What did the hockey coach say when they won the championship?
- "We really 'iced' the competition!"

13. How do you know if a coach is a good storyteller?
- The players are all ears!

14. Why did the mentor take their hockey team to the bakery?
- To work on their "roll" models!

15. How do you describe a hockey coach's favorite vacation?
- A trip to "Win-ipeg!"

7. WOMEN IN CANADIAN HOCKEY

- **Hayley Wickenheiser: A Trailblazer**
- **Marie-Philip Poulin: Golden Moments**
- **Leading the Way for Female Players**

HAYLEY WICKENHEISER: A TRAILBLAZER

1. Early Start:
- Hayley Wickenheiser began playing hockey at age five, displaying her passion for the sport from a young age.

2. Multi-Sport Athlete:
- In addition to her impressive hockey career, Wickenheiser is also recognized as a talented multi-sport athlete. She has achieved high levels of success in softball as well.

3. Olympic Star:
- In addition to playing hockey, Wickenheiser is known for her versatility as a multi-sport athlete. She has also excelled in softball at a high level.

4. Medical Career:
- Besides her athletic accomplishments, Hayley pursued a medical profession. She studied kinesiology with the aim of becoming an ER doctor.

5. Men's Professional Hockey:
- Wickenheiser made history by playing professional men's hockey in Finland, breaking gender barriers and inspiring future generations.

6. Order of Canada:
- In 2011, Hayley Wickenheiser was appointed to the Order of Canada in recognition of her contributions to Canadian sports and leadership.

7. Youth Mentorship:
- Hayley is an active mentor and advocate for women in sports, promoting increased opportunities for young athletes.

8. Hockey Hall of Fame:
- Wickenheiser was inducted into the Hockey Hall of Fame in 2019, solidifying her status as one of the greatest hockey players of all time.

9. Philanthropy:
- She uses her influence to support healthcare and youth development initiatives.

10. Leadership Roles:
- Hayley Wickenheiser has become a leader in hockey administration, contributing to the growth and development of the sport at all levels.

Hayley Wickenheiser

By Simon Fraser University - University Communications - Hayley Wickenheiser, CC BY 2.0, https://commons.wikimedia.org/w/index.php?curid=40610909

MARIE-PHILIP POULIN: GOLDEN MOMENTS

1. Two-Time Olympic Hero:
- Marie-Philip Poulin scored game-winning goals in the 2010 and 2014 Olympic women's hockey finals, securing her place in Canadian sports history.

2. Young Achiever:
- Poulin made her debut on the Canadian national team at the young age of 18, where she showcased her impressive talent and composure on the ice.

3. Captaincy:
- She led the Canadian women's national team with skill and determination as their captain.

4. Professional Success:
- Poulin has had success in professional women's hockey leagues, contributing to the growth and visibility of the sport beyond international competition.

5. World Championship Achievements:
- Beyond the Olympics, Poulin has excelled in the IIHF Women's World Championships, helping Canada secure gold in multiple tournaments.

6. University Hockey Star:
- Before achieving international success, Poulin had an outstanding career in Canadian university hockey, earning recognition for her skills and sportsmanship.

7. Inspiring the Next Generation:
- Marie-Philip Poulin actively encourages young girls to pursue their dreams in hockey, emphasizing the importance of hard work and dedication.

8. Impactful Playmaker:
- Known for her playmaking skills, Poulin is a skilled scorer and passer, contributing to her team's success.

9. Montreal Canadiennes:
- Poulin played for the Montreal Canadiennes in the Canadian Women's Hockey League, establishing herself as a prominent figure in the sport.

10. Continued Dominance:
- Recently, Poulin has continued to dominate women's hockey by showcasing her skill and leadership on the international stage.

Marie-Philip Poulin
By Courtney from Vancouver, Canada - Melodie Daoust, CC BY 2.0,
https://commons.wikimedia.org/w/index.php?curid=113048935

LEADING THE WAY FOR FEMALE PLAYERS

1. Angela James:
- Angela James, known as the "Wayne Gretzky of women's hockey," paved the way for future generations with exceptional skill and dedication.

2. Manon Rhéaume:
- Manon Rhéaume broke gender barriers by playing in an NHL exhibition game.

3. Development of Women's Leagues:
- Female hockey players, such as Jayna Hefford and Cassie Campbell-Pascall, played pivotal roles in developing women's hockey leagues, contributing to increased opportunities for women in the sport.

4. Impact of the CWHL:
- The Canadian Women's Hockey League (CWHL) provided a professional platform for female hockey players.

5. Emergence of the NWHL:
- The National Women's Hockey League (NWHL) is a significant contributor to the growth of professional women's hockey.

6. Ongoing Advocacy:
- Female hockey players have been advocating for gender equality in the sport, seeking better resources, visibility, and opportunities for women.

7. Youth Development Programs:
- Several programs and initiatives exist to encourage young girls to participate in hockey, thereby fostering the growth of women's hockey.

8. Global Competitors:
- Canadian female hockey players have been instrumental in raising the level of competition in the international women's hockey community.

9. Impact Beyond the Rink:
- Female players have made significant contributions beyond the rink, becoming leaders, mentors, and advocates for positive societal change.

10. Olympic Showcases:
- The inclusion of women's hockey in the Olympics has been instrumental in showcasing the skill and athleticism of female players on a global stage.

Cherie Piper

By Krista Windsor - DSC_0761, CC BY-SA 2.0, https://commons.wikimedia.org/w/index.php?curid=50733393

TRIVIA QUIZ 7

HAYLEY WICKENHEISER: A TRAILBLAZER

1. What notable achievement did Hayley Wickenheiser accomplish by playing professional men's hockey in Finland?
   - A. First female coach in men's hockey
   - B. First female to win a men's league scoring title
   - C. First female to captain a men's professional team

2. In addition to her hockey career, what field did Hayley Wickenheiser pursue academically?
   - A. Law
   - B. Medicine
   - C. Engineering

3. How many consecutive Olympic Games did Hayley Wickenheiser score in, making her the first Canadian to do so?
   - A. Four
   - B. Five
   - C. Six

4. What prestigious recognition did Hayley Wickenheiser receive in 2019, acknowledging her impact on the sport?
   - A. Olympic Gold Medal
   - B. Hockey Hall of Fame induction
   - C. Order of Canada

5. Apart from playing, how does Hayley Wickenheiser contribute to the development of young athletes?
- A. Youth mentorship programs
- B. Hockey coaching clinics
- C. Sports psychology seminars

MARIE-PHILIP POULIN: GOLDEN MOMENTS

1. What nickname is Marie-Philip Poulin often referred to after her clutch performances in Olympic gold medal games?

- A. Golden Girl
- B. Captain Clutch
- C. The Ice Queen

2. Before her international success, in which league did Marie-Philip Poulin have a standout career?
- A. Professional Women's Hockey League (PWHL)
- B. Canadian Women's Hockey League (CWHL)
- C. Canadian Interuniversity Sport (CIS)

3. In which years did Marie-Philip Poulin score the game-winning goals in the Olympic gold medal women's hockey finals?
- A. 2010 and 2014
- B. 2014 and 2018
- C. 2006 and 2010

4. What leadership role has Marie-Philip Poulin taken on for the Canadian women's national team?
- A. Head Coach
- B. Team Captain
- C. Goalie Coach

5. Besides her Olympic success, in which professional women's hockey league has Marie-Philip Poulin continued to excel?
   - A. National Women's Hockey League (NWHL)
   - B. Premier Hockey Federation (PHF)
   - C. European Women's Hockey League (EWHL)

LEADING THE WAY FOR FEMALE PLAYERS

1. Who is often referred to as the "Wayne Gretzky of women's hockey" for her pioneering contributions to the sport?
   - A. Angela James
   - B. Manon Rhéaume
   - C. Jayna Hefford

2. What historic milestone did Manon Rhéaume achieve in the NHL, breaking gender barriers?
   - A. First female NHL coach
   - B. First female to win the Stanley Cup
   - C. First female to play in an NHL exhibition game

3. Which Canadian female players played pivotal roles in the development of women's hockey leagues?
   - A. Angela James and Cassie Campbell-Pascall
   - B. Hayley Wickenheiser and Jayna Hefford
   - C. Marie-Philip Poulin and Manon Rhéaume

4. What was the impact of the Canadian Women's Hockey League (CWHL) on women's hockey?
   - A. It disbanded in 2019
   - B. It merged with the National Women's Hockey League (NWHL)
   - C. It was the first professional women's hockey league

5. Besides their contributions on the ice, how have female players like Hayley Wickenheiser and Jayna Hefford made a positive impact?
   1. A. By writing books on hockey
   2. B. Through youth mentorship and advocacy
   3. C. By founding their own hockey equipment brands

HAYLEY WICKENHEISER: A TRAILBLAZER

1. Why did Hayley Wickenheiser bring a ladder to the hockey game?
Because she wanted to reach new heights on the ice!

2 What did the hockey puck say to Hayley Wickenheiser?
"You can't catch me; I'm on the Wickenheiser fast track!"

3. Why did Hayley Wickenheiser become a doctor after her hockey career?
Because she wanted to heal the competition!

4. How does Hayley Wickenheiser stay cool during intense hockey moments?
She has a Wicken-chill attitude!

5. What did Hayley Wickenheiser say when she scored the winning goal?
"Just Wicken-awesome, as usual!"

JOKE TIME

MARIE-PHILIP POULIN: GOLDEN MOMENTS

1. Why did Marie-Philip Poulin bring a broom to the hockey rink?
   - Because she's always sweeping up the competition!

2. What's Marie-Philip Poulin's favorite type of goal?
   - The "golden" one, of course!

3. How does Marie-Philip Poulin celebrate a hockey victory?
   - With a "golden" dance in the locker room!

4. What did Marie-Philip Poulin say when asked about her incredible goals?
   - "I guess you could say I have a 'golden' touch!"

5. How does Marie-Philip Poulin take her coffee?
   - "Golden" with a dash of victory!

87

JOKE TIME

LEADING THE WAY FOR FEMALE PLAYERS

1. Why did Angela James bring a map to the hockey game?
- She wanted to show everyone the route to success!

2. How does Manon Rhéaume like her ice cream?
- In a historic cone that breaks the gender barrier!

3. What's the favorite dessert of female players who led the way in hockey?
- Breakthrough brownies!

4. Why did female players start a comedy club?
- To score laughs and break the ice in the hockey world!

5. What's the secret to success for leading female players in hockey?
- A combination of skill, determination, and a good sense of humor!

8. MOST EXCITING MATCHES

- 1972 Summit Series: Canada vs. the Soviet Union
- Mario's Miracle: The 1987 Canada Cup Showdown
- The Golden Moment: 2010 Winter Olympics
- 2014 Sochi Olympics Men's Hockey Final
- 2016 World Cup of Hockey Final: Canada vs. Team Europe
- 2020 IIHF World Junior Championship Final: Canada vs. Russia

1972 SUMMIT SERIES: CANADA VS. THE SOVIET UNION

1. During the 1972 Summit Series, Canada and the Soviet Union played an unforgettable eight-game hockey match.

2. Paul Henderson scored the winning goal in the final moments of Game 8, securing Canada's victory and earning himself a permanent place in hockey history.

3. The Summit Series was a significant moment in international hockey, as it demonstrated the talent and competitiveness of both Canadian and Soviet players.

MARIO'S MIRACLE: THE 1987 CANADA CUP SHOWDOWN

4. The 1987 Canada Cup is well-known for Mario Lemieux's remarkable and game-winning goal in the decisive game against the Soviet Union.

5. This goal, which was assisted by Wayne Gretzky, is often referred to as "Mario's Miracle" and is considered one of the most significant moments in Canadian hockey history.

Mario Lemieux- Hall of Fame

By Spoutnik33 from french Wikipédia. - Own work, CC BY-SA 3.0, https://commons.wikimedia.org/w/index.php?curid=2824080

THE GOLDEN MOMENT: 2010 WINTER OLYMPICS

6. At the 2010 Winter Olympics in Vancouver, Sidney Crosby scored the "Golden Goal" in overtime, which led Canada to victory over the United States.

7. The triumph of winning the gold medal on their home soil filled Canadians with immense pride, and the moment is forever cherished in the hearts of hockey fans across the country.

2014 SOCHI OLYMPICS MEN'S HOCKEY FINAL

8. Canada's men's hockey team, captained by Sidney Crosby, won gold at the 2014 Sochi Olympics.

9. They defeated Sweden 3-0 in the final with a stellar defensive performance and shutout by goaltender Carey Price.

By Atos - Atos at the Olympic Winter Games Ice Hockey - Was it really a score or not- Russia againts Slovenia - score 4-2Uploaded by Sporti, CC BY-SA 2.0, https://commons.wikimedia.org/w/index.php?curid=31161555

2016 WORLD CUP OF HOCKEY FINAL: CANADA VS. TEAM EUROPE

10. The 2016 World Cup of Hockey marked the tournament's return after a 12-year break.

11. Canada won 2-1 against Team Europe in the final to become champions.

2020 IIHF WORLD JUNIOR CHAMPIONSHIP FINAL: CANADA VS. RUSSIA

12. The final match of the 2020 IIHF World Junior Championship was between Canada's junior hockey team and Russia.

13. Akil Thomas scored the game-winning goal, securing Canada's gold medal and adding another thrilling chapter to the nation's junior hockey legacy.

ADDITIONAL FACTS

14. Wayne Gretzky holds numerous records, including the most career goals and points in NHL history.

15. The Hockey Hall of Fame in Toronto honors the game's greatest players, coaches, and builders.

16. Canada is the birthplace of ice hockey, with early versions of the game played in Nova Scotia in the 1800s.

17. The Stanley Cup, awarded to the NHL champion, is North America's oldest professional sports trophy.

18. The Molson Canadian World Hockey Summit in 2010 brought together hockey experts to discuss the state and future of the game.

19. The IIHF World Women's Championship showcases the best women's hockey teams worldwide.

20. The Clarkson Cup is the championship trophy for the Canadian Women's Hockey League (CWHL), celebrating excellence in women's hockey.

TRIVIA QUIZ 8

1972 SUMMIT SERIES: CANADA VS. THE SOVIET UNION

1. In the 1972 Summit Series, how many games were played between Canada and the Soviet Union?
- A. 5
- B. 6
- C. 8

2. Who scored the game-winning goal in the final moments of Game 8 in the 1972 Summit Series?
- A. Wayne Gretzky
- B. Paul Henderson
- C. Bobby Orr

MARIO'S MIRACLE: THE 1987 CANADA CUP SHOWDOWN

3. What is the iconic moment in the 1987 Canada Cup referred to as?
- A. Gretzky's Glory
- B. Mario's Miracle
- C. The Great Showdown

4: Who scored the dramatic and game-winning goal in the 1987 Canada Cup final?
- A. Wayne Gretzky
- B. Mario Lemieux
- C. Mark Messier

THE GOLDEN MOMENT: 2010 WINTER OLYMPICS

5: In the 2010 Winter Olympics, which Canadian player scored the "Golden Goal" in overtime?
- A. Sidney Crosby
- B. Jonathan Toews
- C. Ryan Getzlaf

6: Where were the 2010 Winter Olympics held?
- A. Vancouver
- B. Sochi
- C. Salt Lake City

2014 SOCHI OLYMPICS MEN'S HOCKEY FINAL

7: Who captained the Canadian men's hockey team to gold at the 2014 Sochi Olympics?
- A. Sidney Crosby
- B. Jonathan Toews
- C. Shea Weber

8: What was the final score in the 2014 Sochi Olympics men's hockey final, where Canada defeated Sweden?
- A. 3-0
- B. 3-1
- C. 4-2

2016 WORLD CUP OF HOCKEY FINAL: CANADA VS. TEAM EUROPE

9: The 2016 World Cup of Hockey marked the return of the tournament after how many years?
- A. 6
- B. 8
- C. 12

10: Who coached Team Canada to victory in the 2016 World Cup of Hockey?
- A. Mike Babcock
- B. Joel Quenneville
- C. Claude Julien

2020 IIHF WORLD JUNIOR CHAMPIONSHIP FINAL: CANADA VS. RUSSIA

11: In the 2020 IIHF World Junior Championship, where was the final held between Canada and Russia?
- A. Helsinki
- B. Edmonton
- C. Stockholm

12: Who scored the game-winning goal for Canada in the 2020 IIHF World Junior Championship final against Russia?
- A. Alexis Lafrenière
- B. Dylan Cozens
- C. Akil Thomas

JOKE TIME

1. Why did the hockey puck want to be part of the 1972 Summit Series?
Because it heard it was the coolest event on ice!

2 How did the Soviet goalie prepare for the Summit Series?
By staying cool under the Red pressure!

3. Why did Mario Lemieux bring a map to the 1987 Canada Cup?
He wanted to find the quickest route to the Miracle on Ice!

4. What did Wayne Gretzky say to Mario Lemieux after his game-winning goal?
"You really know how to 'goal' above and beyond!"

5. How did Sidney Crosby feel after scoring the Golden Goal?
On top of the world – or at least on top of the podium!

6. Why did the hockey puck attend the 2010 Winter Olympics?
To witness the ultimate golden touch!

7. How did the Canadian goalie keep warm in the Sochi Olympics final?
By turning away the Swedish shots and staying hot on ice!

8. Why did the Swedish players bring extra sweaters to the Sochi final?
- They knew Canada had a chilling defense!

Joke Time

9. What did the World Cup of Hockey say to Canada?
- "You're my favorite team, and I'm not just puck-ering up!"

10. How did Team Europe feel after facing Canada in the final?
- Like they went through a world of hockey emotions – and Canada was the champion at the end!

11. Why did the Canadian player bring a ladder to the 2020 IIHF World Junior Championship Final?
- To reach new heights and score goals above the competition!

12. How did the hockey players stay warm during the cold 2020 IIHF World Junior Championship?
- By playing so hot that the ice melted around them!

13. Why did the female hockey player bring a dictionary to the game?
- To check the meaning of "slapshot" – she wanted to be on the same page as the puck!

TRIVIA QUIZ 1

1. Montreal, Quebec.
2. Wood.
3. Canada.
4. Shinny.
5. Bandy.
6. A small ball.
7. Barrel staves or wooden posts.
8. Fiberglass and composite materials.
9. Shinty.
10. 1920.
11. December 19, 1917.
12. Any three out of: Montreal Canadiens, Toronto Maple Leafs, Boston Bruins, Chicago Blackhawks, Detroit Red Wings, New York Rangers.
13. James Creighton.
14. Alberta.
15. England.
16. The Stanley Cup.
17. Montreal Canadiens.
18. Toronto, Ontario.
19. Canada and Russia.
20. 1990.

Wayne Gretzky: The Great One

1. 1979 (He played for four NHL teams from 1979 to 1999: the Edmonton Oilers, Los Angeles Kings, St. Louis Blues, and New York Rangers.)
2. 99.
3. Los Angeles Kings.
4. The Great One.
5. Four.

Bobby Orr: A Defenseman's Dream

6. Boston Bruins.
7. Orr soaring through the air.
8. Eight.
9. "The Bobby Orr Rule" restricted goaltenders' puck handling beyond the crease.
10. The Boston Bruins retired jersey number 4 to honor Bobby Orr.

Maurice "Rocket" Richard: Scoring Sensation

11. Rocket.
12. 1944-45.
13. Eight.
14. Richard's suspension resulted from an on-ice altercation with a linesman
15. The Montreal Canadiens retired jersey number 9 to honor Maurice Richard.

The Quest for Lord Stanley's Cup

1. Sir Frederick Arthur Stanley.
2. Bowl-like.
3. 1926.
4. : Keeper of the Cup.
5. Lord Stanley of Preston.
6. Engraving the names of winning teams and players.
7. Multiple leagues.
8. Used as a flower pot, thrown into a canal, and left at the side of the road.
9. Stanley Cup Ring.
10. Stanley Cup Trust.

Historic Stanley Cup Moments

1. 1936.
2. Bill Mosienko.
3. 1942-1967.
4. Wayne Gretzky.
5. Jacques Plante.
6. Wayne Gretzky.
7. Sidney Crosby.
8. Newsy Lalonde.
9. 1942 Toronto Maple Leafs and 1975 New York Islanders.
10. Six.

Canadian Dominance in the NHL

1. 1942-1967.
2. Edmonton Oilers.
3. 24.
4. Canadian Triple Crown.
5. Immeasurable.
6. Patrick Roy, Martin Brodeur, Terry Sawchuk.
7. A significant number.
8. Toronto Maple Leafs.
9. Battle of Alberta (Calgary Flames vs. Edmonton Oilers).
10. Edmonton Oilers.

TRIVIA QUIZ 4

Kid Heroes of the NHL

1. Three.
2. Connor McDavid.
3. San Ramon, California.
4. Eight.
5. Mathew Barzal.

Bobby Orr: A Defenseman's Dream

6. 1979-80.
7. Bobby Orr.
8. 76 goals.
9. 102.
10. Patrick Kane.

Maurice "Rocket" Richard: Scoring Sensation

11. The Russian Rocket.
12. Guy Lafleur.
13. Early years with the Edmonton Oilers.
14. 41.
15. Daniel and Henrik Sedin.

Backyard Rinks and Frozen Ponds

1. Best backyard rink contests.
2. Intricate designs and patterns..
3. Modified lawnmowers.
4. Winter wildlife..
5. Hot chocolate, bonfires, and shared winter activities.

Learning to Skate and Shoot

6. Snow-covered driveways.
7. Coaches.
8. Snowbanks.
9. Pucks slapping against the ice..
10. Quick shooting sessions.

From Pick-Up Games to Organized Hockey

11. On frozen ponds.
12. The transition from casual games to structured competition.
13. Frozen lakesides.
14. Feature pick-up games.
15. Hockey moms.

Values and Traditions of the Game

1. "The Hockey Sweater."
2. The Molson Cup.
3. Montreal Canadiens, Toronto Maple Leafs, Boston Bruins, Chicago Blackhawks, Detroit Red Wings, and New York Rangers.
4. "Hockey Night in Canada."
5. An outdoor NHL game celebrating the roots of the sport, often played in iconic Canadian settings.

Sportsmanship and Teamwork

1. An outdoor NHL game celebrating the roots of the sport, often played in iconic Canadian settings.
2. Team captains.
3. Donate money to charity.
4. Swapping jerseys after a game.
5. Tap their sticks on the ice.

The Role of Coaches and Mentors

1. Scotty Bowman.
2. Pat Quinn.
3. The Jack Adams Award.
4. Herb Brooks.
5. The enduring influence of mentorship in hockey.

TRIVIA QUIZ 7

Hayley Wickenheiser: A Trailblazer

1. B. First female to win a men's league scoring title
2. B. Medicine
3. B. Five
4. B. Hockey Hall of Fame induction
5. A. Youth mentorship programs

Marie-Philip Poulin: Golden Moments

1. B. Captain Clutch
2. C. Canadian Interuniversity Sport (CIS)
3. A. 2010 and 2014
4. B. Team Captain
5. B. Premier Hockey Federation (PHF)

Leading the Way for Female Players

1. A. Angela James
2. C. First female to play in an NHL exhibition game
3. A. Angela James and Cassie Campbell-Pascall
4. A. It disbanded in 2019
5. B. Through youth mentorship and advocacy

1972 Summit Series: Canada vs. the Soviet Union

1. C. 8
2. B. Paul Henderson

Mario's Miracle: The 1987 Canada Cup Showdown

3. B. Mario's Miracle
4. B. Mario Lemieux

The Golden Moment: 2010 Winter Olympics

5. A. Sidney Crosby
6. A. Vancouver

2014 Sochi Olympics Men's Hockey Final

7. A. Sidney Crosby
8. A. 3-0

2016 World Cup of Hockey Final: Canada vs. Team Europe
9. C. 12
10. A. Mike Babcock

2016 World Cup of Hockey Final: Canada vs. Team Europe

11. B. Edmonton
12. C. Akil Thomas

CONCLUSION

This book celebrates the sport of hockey in Canadian culture, from its humble beginnings to the feats of legends like Wayne Gretzky and Maurice "Rocket" Richard. The Stanley Cup is a testament to the perseverance and excellence of Canadian teams. Through heroes and stories, hockey has become vital to Canadian identity, whether on backyard rinks, in arenas, or through coaches and mentors.

The spirit of Canadian hockey, with its values, traditions, and the camaraderie that transcends the ice, has been a guiding force throughout our journey. The emergence of women in Canadian hockey, led by trailblazers like Hayley Wickenheiser and Marie-Philip Poulin, showcases the evolving and inclusive nature of the sport.

As we relive the most exciting matches in Canadian hockey history, we feel the pulse of a nation united by the love for the game.

This book includes trivia, fun facts, and jokes to make Canadian hockey more enjoyable and informative. We hope this book will be your companion on your journey through the exciting world of hockey.

In Canadian hockey, the final buzzer only marks the end of one chapter, and the beginning of a new one is just a slapshot away. Keep the passion alive, and enjoy the joy of Canadian hockey forever.

Dr. Fanatomy

OTHER BOOKS

Please let us know how we're doing by leaving us a review.

Made in United States
Troutdale, OR
12/20/2024